Mighty Machines
CARS

Ian Graham

QED Publishing

Copyright © QED Publishing 2008

First published in the UK in 2008 by
QED Publishing
A Quarto Group company
226 City Road
London EC1V 2TT

www.qed-publishing.co.uk

A Catalogue record for this book is available from the British Library.

ISBN 978 1 84538 927 7

Written by Ian Graham
Designer Phil and Traci Morash
Editor Paul Manning
Picture Researcher Claudia Tate

Publisher Steve Evans
Creative Director Zeta Davies
Editorial Manager Wendy Horobin

Printed and bound in China

Picture credits
Key: t = top, FC = front cover

BMW/4, 14; **Corbis**/George Tiedemann/GT Images 12, /Mazen Mahdi/epa 13t, /David Cooper/
Toronto Star/ZUMA 15t, /Don Mason 16, /Alex Hofford/epa 20, /Brooks Kraft 21t; **Getty Images**/18;
GM UK & Ireland/9t; **Rex**/Paul Cooper FC; **Shutterstock**/Joseph Gareri 5t, /Toyota (GB) PLC 6,
/Richard Foreman 7t, /Julie Lucht 8, /Anatoliy Meshkov 10, /Maserati S.p.A. 11t, /Mikolaj Tomczak 17t,
/Losevsky Pavel 19.

Words in **bold** can be found
in the Glossary on page 23.

Contents

What is a car?

The job of a car is to carry us from place to place. Every car has an **engine**. The engine burns **fuel** and provides power to turn the wheels.

boot

The **boot** at the back of the car is for carrying things.

A car's engine is a complicated machine with hundreds of moving parts. Slippery oil keeps them all moving easily.

bonnet

In most cars, the engine is at the front, underneath the **bonnet**.

Everyday **cars**

Cars are made in all shapes and sizes. Small cars, or **compacts**, are good for short journeys. Business people who drive long distances prefer bigger cars with more powerful engines.

A car like this would suit a family with two small children.

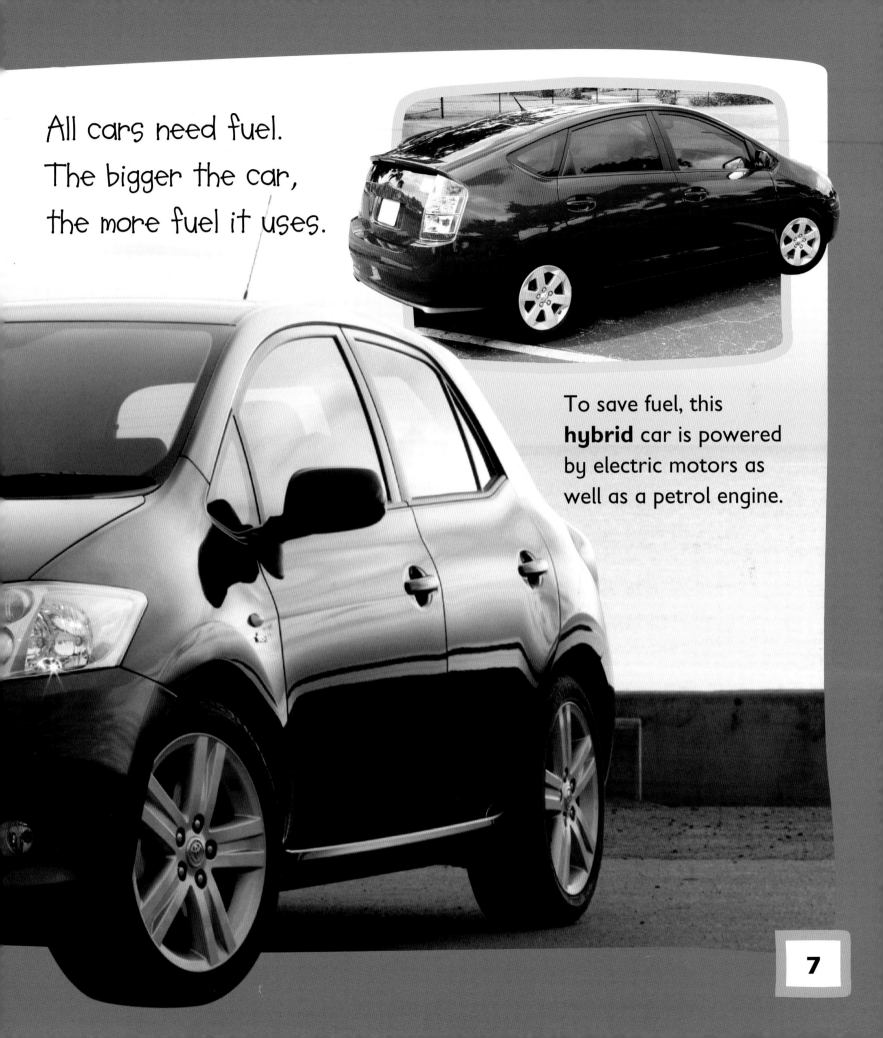

All cars need fuel.
The bigger the car,
the more fuel it uses.

To save fuel, this **hybrid** car is powered by electric motors as well as a petrol engine.

Sports **cars**

Sports cars are designed to be fun to drive. They are small, lightweight, **manoeuvrable** – and fast!

Some sports cars have a top that can be folded down or taken off completely if the weather is fine. This type of car is called a convertible.

The low, smooth shape of this car helps it to go faster by letting air flow easily over it.

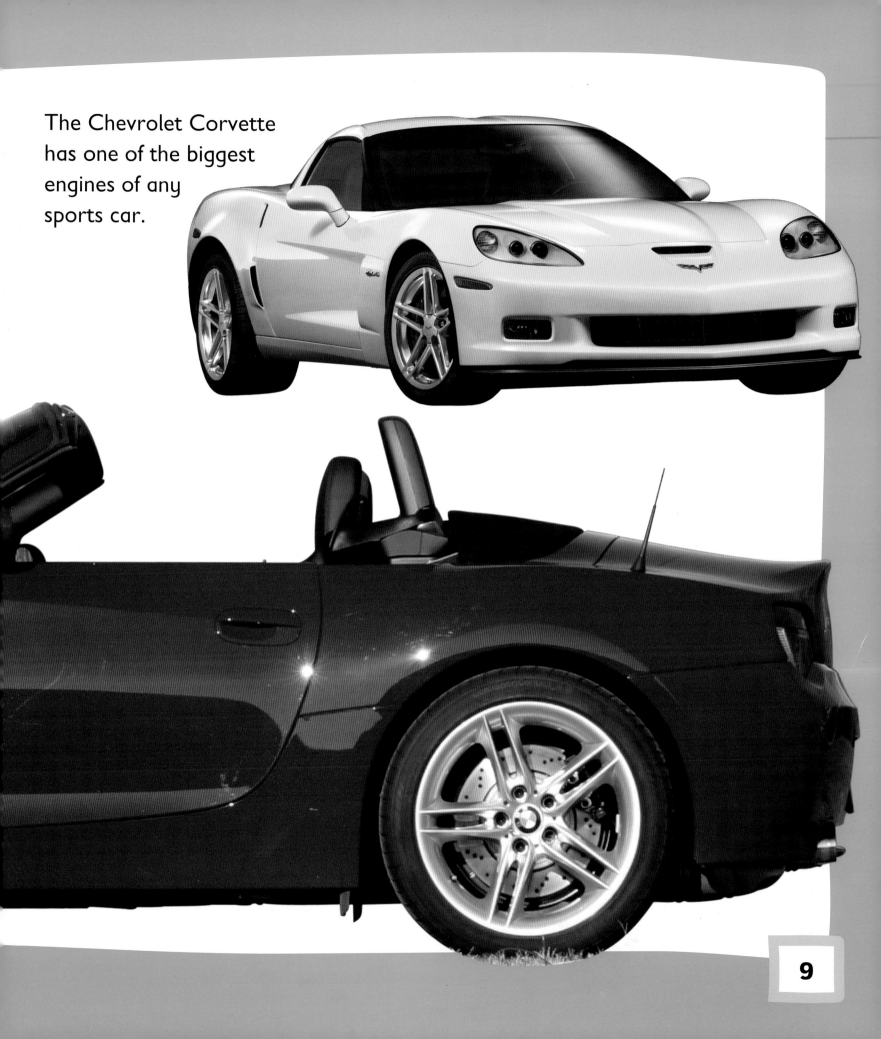

The Chevrolet Corvette has one of the biggest engines of any sports car.

Supercars

Supercars are the most powerful sports cars allowed on the roads. Some supercars have engines so big that they are like two ordinary car engines side by side!

air vent

This Ferrari Enzo has a top speed of 350 kilometres an hour. Vents at the front and side take in air to feed its massive engine.

The Maserati MC12 is built like a racing car, with the engine behind the driver to spread the weight.

Supercars are designed to be the best, whatever the cost. Only a few of these amazing cars are ever built.

On the race track

Motor-racing is one of the most **popular** and exciting sports. All sorts of cars can take part. As well as specially built racing cars, there are races for sports cars and even family cars.

These NASCAR cars are the same shape as ordinary cars, but each is a hand-built racer with a top speed of 320 kilometres an hour.

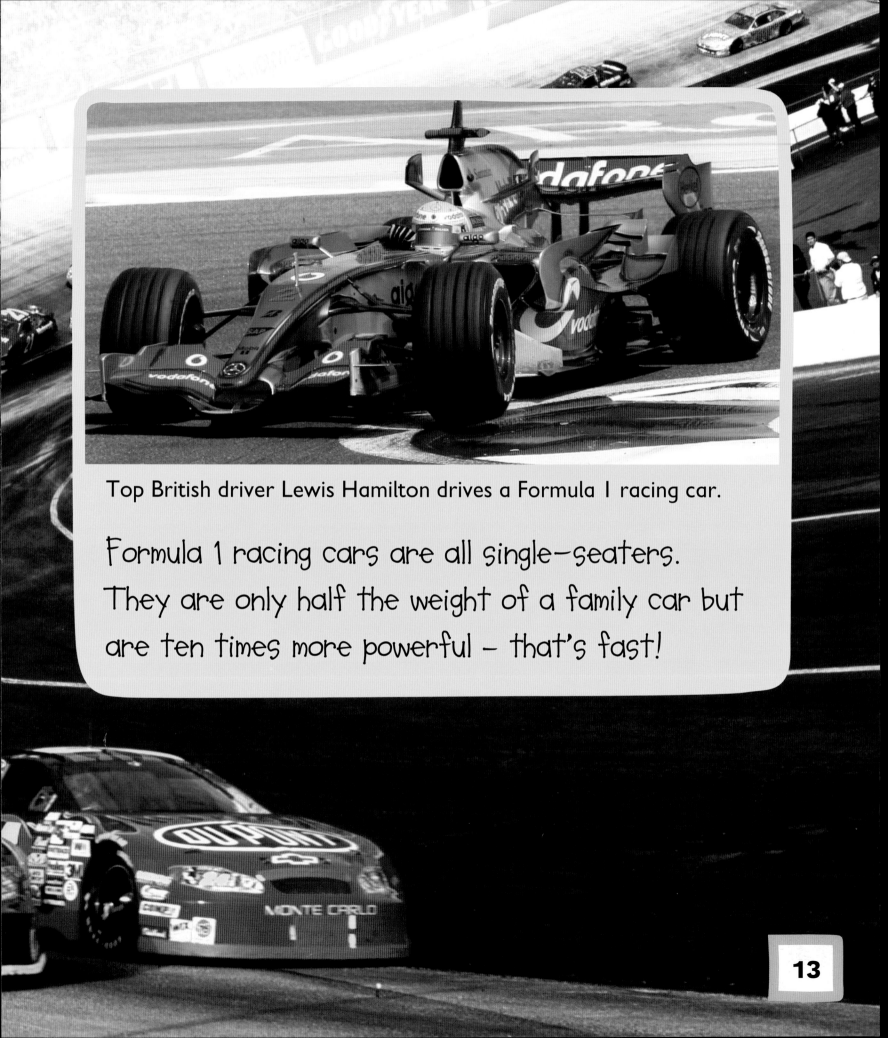

Top British driver Lewis Hamilton drives a Formula 1 racing car.

Formula 1 racing cars are all single-seaters. They are only half the weight of a family car but are ten times more powerful – that's fast!

In the city

City cars that are used mostly for short journeys do not need to be big and powerful. In fact, the smaller they are, the better!

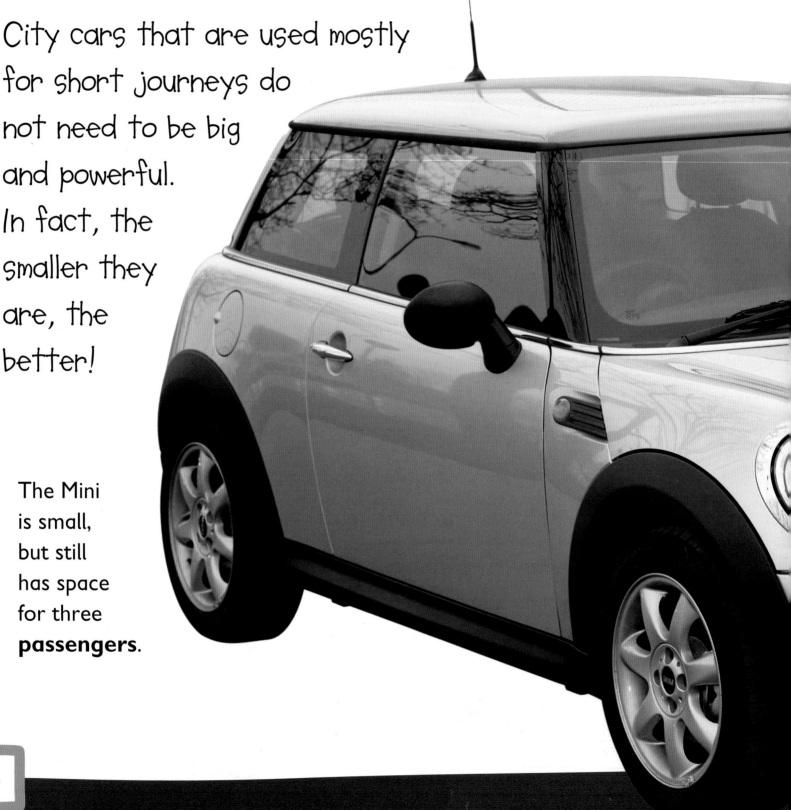

The Mini is small, but still has space for three **passengers**.

In towns and cities, smaller cars are a lot easier to park. They can squeeze into spaces where bigger cars will not fit.

This city car is so short that it can even be parked sideways.

Carrying more

People carriers, or MPVs (multi-purpose **vehicles**), have more space for passengers than ordinary cars.

The seats of an MPV are raised to give the driver and passengers a better view of the road. The back seats fold down easily to make extra carrying space.

This **mini-MPV** is just the right size and shape for carrying emergency medical supplies.

This roomy MPV has eight seats and still has space for the shopping!

Going off-road

When the going gets tough, the car you need is an SUV (Sports Utility Vehicle).

With their chunky tyres, SUVs can easily drive over rough or muddy ground without getting stuck. The engine also powers all four wheels, to give more grip on mud, snow and ice.

Only a **four-by-four** could plough through ground as wet and muddy as this!

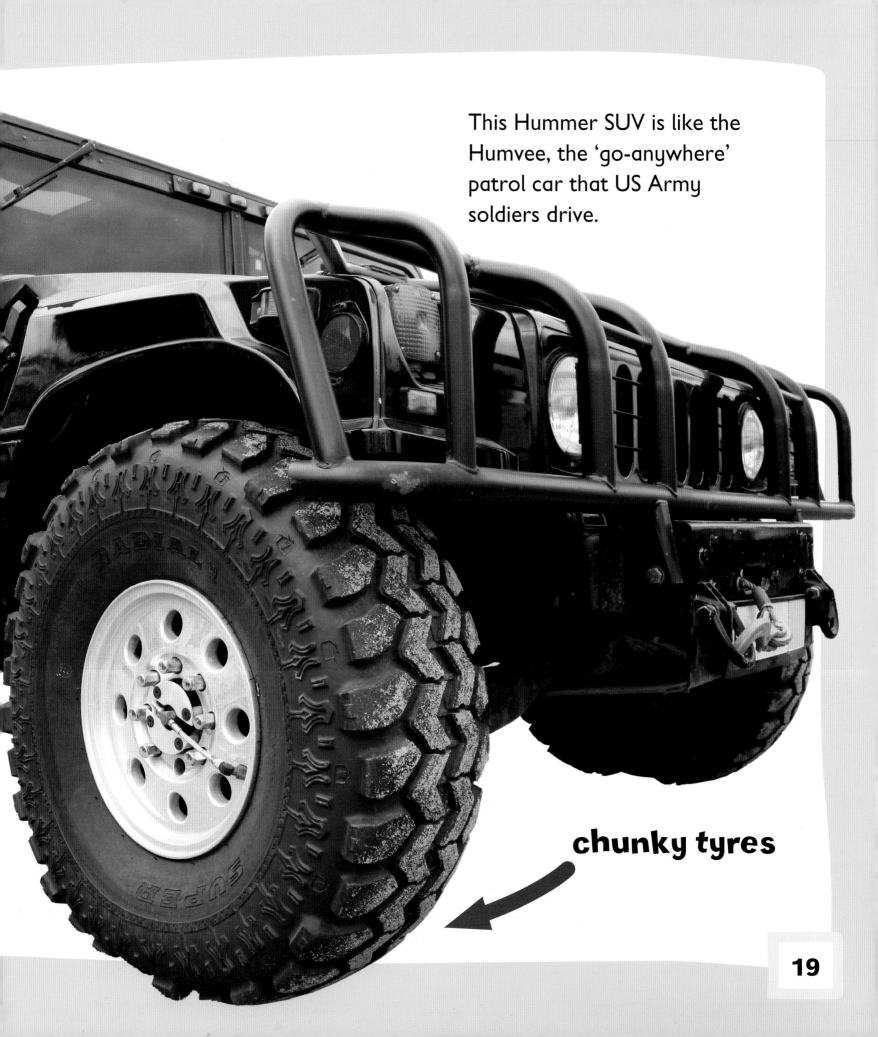

This Hummer SUV is like the Humvee, the 'go-anywhere' patrol car that US Army soldiers drive.

chunky tyres

Luxury cars

If you want to travel in real comfort, try a limousine!

Limousines are mostly for important people, such as presidents or kings and queens. But they can be fun to hire for special occasions, such as weddings, too.

The US president travels in this specially adapted Cadillac. The body is **armour-plated** and the windows are made of bulletproof glass for protection.

Extra-long luxury cars are called stretch limos. The longest stretch limos have five doors on each side and seats for up to ten passengers!

Rolls-Royce is a famous maker of luxury cars.

Activities

- What sort of cars are these?

- Draw your own car and make up a story about it. What sort of car is it? Where is it going, and why? Who is travelling in it?

- Make a collection of pictures of different kinds of cars from magazines and comics. How many types can you find?

- If you had to drive along a muddy road, would a sports car or an SUV be better? Which car would you choose, and why?

- Which of these cars would be driven by a racing driver?

Glossary

Armour-plated
Specially strengthened to protect against bullets or missiles

Bonnet
The part of a car's body at the front that protects the engine

Boot
Space at the back of a car for carrying things

Compact
A type of car suitable for a small family

Engine
The machine inside a car that provides power to make the wheels go round

Four-by-four
A car in which the engine drives all four wheels, not just the two at the front or back

Fuel
The liquid burned inside a car engine to make it go. Most car engines burn petrol or diesel

Hybrid
A car that saves fuel by using electric motors as well as a petrol engine to drive the wheels

Manoeuvrable
Easy to steer or control

Mini-MPV
An MPV with fewer seats but a tall space behind for carrying things

Popular
Liked by a lot of people

Passengers
The people who travel in a car as well as the driver

Vehicle
A machine with an engine that carries people or things

Index